A ROOKIE BIOGRAPHY

BLACK ELK

A Man with a Vision

By Carol Greene

CHILDRENS PRESS®
CHICAGO

This book is for Clifford H. Greene.

Black Elk (1863-1950)

Library of Congress Cataloging-in-Publication Data

Greene, Carol.
    Black Elk : (a man with a vision) / by Carol Greene.
      p. cm. — (A Rookie biography)
    Includes index.
    Summary: A simple account of the life of Black Elk, the visionary and
Oglala medicine man who has a vision of universal peace and felt that he
saw his people's dream die at Wounded Knee.
    ISBN 0-516-04213-0
    1. Black Elk, 1863-1950—Juvenile literature. 2. Oglala Indians—
Biography—Juvenile literature. 3. Oglala Indians—Religion and
mythology—Juvenile literature. [1. Black Elk, 1863-1950. 2. Oglala
Indians—Biography. 3. Indians of North America—Biography.] I. Title.
II. Series: Greene, Carol. Rookie biography.
E99.03B534   1990
973'.0497502—dc20
[B]
[92]   90-39480
                                                CIP
                                                AC

Black Elk was
a real person.
He was born in 1863.
He died in 1950.
Black Elk had a vision
of the whole earth
living in peace.
This is his story.

TABLE OF CONTENTS

The Black Hills (above) are in South Dakota. The buffalo (below) gave the Indians food, clothing, and shelter.

Chapter 1

The Great Vision

Black Elk played
near his family's tepee.
He was an Oglala Sioux
from the Black Hills.

The Black Hills were
a good place to live.
The Indians loved the land.
They took care of it,
and the land gave them
all they needed.

An Indian village

But the grown-ups said
that white soldiers were coming.
Black Elk's mother told him
to stay near their tepee.
Black Elk was three years old.
He felt afraid.

The Indians fought the soldiers on horseback.

Later, he learned that
the white men wanted gold
from the Black Hills.
They didn't care about
the land or the Indians
who lived there.

Black Elk's father
went with other Indians
to fight the soldiers.
The Indians won.
But there were more soldiers.
They would come again.

The Indians held horse races (above) and played a ball
game (below) using sticks that had a net at one end. These
were both learning experiences for young Indian boys.

As Black Elk grew,
he learned to ride a pony.
He learned to hunt,
and he played war games.

Then, when he was nine,
he had a great vision.
A vision is like a dream,
but the person isn't asleep.

In his vision,
Black Elk saw many things.
He saw the sky filled
with dancing horses.
He saw a tepee
with a rainbow door.

A tepee
painted with
scenes from
Black Elk's
great vision.

This drawing of Black Elk's vision shows him standing before the six grandfathers in the rainbow tepee.

He met six grandfathers,
who taught him things
and gave him gifts.

In his vision,
Black Elk went to
the top of a mountain.
He looked down and saw
the whole world—
everything that lives.

In the middle of the world
grew a huge tree
full of flowers.
It was a holy tree.

Then Black Elk knew
that all things must
live together in peace.

In his great vision, Black Elk saw the middle of the world.

Black Elk in the other world

At last, he saw
a spotted eagle.
It flew over him
and took care of him.
Then Black Elk walked
back into his own tepee.

An Indian camp on the plains

"The boy is coming to,"
he heard someone say.

Black Elk's parents said
he had been sick
for 12 days.
But Black Elk felt good.

13

He wanted to tell
about his great vision,
But he was afraid
no one would believe him.
After all, he was only nine.

So Black Elk kept
his great vision
deep inside himself.

Chapter 2

Terrible Times

The white men had promised
Black Elk's people that
they could keep their land
"as long as grass shall grow
and the water flow."

But in just a few years,
they forgot their promise.
They still wanted gold.
When Black Elk was 12,
the trouble began.

Gold-hunters came
to the Black Hills

The Indians had camped
in a big village of tepees
along the Little Bighorn River.
They had fine chiefs—
Sitting Bull, Gall, and
Black Elk's cousin, Crazy Horse.

Sitting Bull

Gall

Colonel George Custer (inset) led an army expedition into the Black Hills in 1874. The soldiers found gold.

This painting shows "Custer's Last Stand" at the battle of the Little Big Horn.

On June 25, 1876,
soldiers attacked the village.
Colonel George Custer
was their leader.
The Indians killed Custer
and over 200 of his men.

The Indians won that battle.
But more soldiers came, and
terrible times lay ahead.

Black Elk's people went
from place to place.
They had almost no food,
and the soldiers followed them.

The Indians were chased by the soldiers through the winter snows.
They had very little food and there was much sickness.

The body of Crazy Horse is taken for burial.

Many Indians grew
tired of fighting.
They sold the Black Hills
to the white men.
Then soldiers tricked
Crazy Horse and he was killed.

That made Black Elk cry.
He began to think
about his vision again.
He thought he should be using it
to help his people.

Even the thunder seemed
to say, "It is time!"
But Black Elk didn't
know what to do,
and that made him feel afraid.

At last, when he was 17,
he told a medicine man
about his vision.
The old man said he must
act it out for his people.

So Black Elk asked
his people to help.
He sang and danced
and acted out parts.
Black Elk prayed,
and everyone felt better.

Black Elk (left)
wore his Indian
costume during
his travels
in Europe
with the Wild
West show.

Black Elk knew he had
done the right thing.
He didn't feel afraid anymore.

The white people killed off the huge buffalo herds. In this
engraving, passengers in a train are shooting the animals.

Chapter 3

A Long Trip

But life was still hard.
Black Elk's people lived
in little gray houses now.
They were often hungry.
White men had killed
all the buffalo.

Black Elk had more visions.
In one, he saw an herb
with blue, white, red,
and yellow flowers.

He saw the spotted eagle, too,
and a big cloud
of crying butterflies.

"These are your people,"
said the eagle.
"You shall help them."

So Black Elk learned
a new way to do that.
He found the herb and
used it to help a sick boy.
From then on, he was
a medicine man.

BUFFALO BILL'S WILD WEST
AND CONGRESS OF ROUGH RIDERS OF THE WORLD.

COL. W. F. CODY
BUFFALO BILL
WILL APPEAR
AT EVERY PERFORMANCE

A CONGRESS OF AMERICAN INDIANS. REPRESENTING VARIOUS TRIBES, CHARACTERS AND PECULIARITIES OF THE WILY DUSKY WARRIORS IN SCENES FROM ACTUAL LIFE GIVING THEIR WEIRD WAR DANCES AND PICTURESQUE STYLE OF HORSEMANSHIP.

Buffalo Bill Cody (right).
His Wild West show included
mock battles with Indians
and demonstrations of
shooting skill.

One day, he got a chance
to join a traveling show.
A white man called
Buffalo Bill Cody ran it.
He wanted Indians to
sing and dance in Europe.

27

Sitting Bull (left), seen here with Buffalo Bill,
also appeared in the Wild West show.

Black Elk said yes.
He wanted to do more
to help his people.
He thought he might learn
some secret way on the trip.

The show went east by train.
Black Elk didn't like the eastern cities.
The lights were so bright
that he couldn't see the stars.
People were mean to each other.
Black Elk felt dead inside.

Aerial view of the Wild West show appearing in Paris, France.

In Europe, he liked
the singing and dancing.
But he was homesick.
One day, he visited
a family in Paris, France.

He was sitting with them
when, all at once,
he had a vision.
In it, a cloud
took him home again.
But he had to come back.

The French family said
he had seemed dead
for three days.
When Buffalo Bill heard
how homesick Black Elk was,
he sent him back to America.

When Black Elk got home,
his mother said
she had dreamed
he came to her on a cloud.
Then he told her
about his vision.

Black Elk was glad
to be home again.
But he felt sad, too.
He had learned no
secret way to help his people.

A Sioux camp in South Dakota in the 1890s. In the scene below, strips of meat are drying on racks outside the tepees.

Chapter 4

The Dream That Died

Black Elk's brother and sister
died while he was gone.
Soon his father died, too.
Black Elk found a job
in a store to get food
for his mother.

Diseases were killing
many of his people.
He could help only a few.

An Indian performs a special dance, called the Ghost Dance, to bring on the new world.

But out west, an Indian holy man
said a new world was coming.
When it came, dead Indians
would be alive again.
There would be buffalo, too.
The Indians must do a dance
and wear shirts with special markings.

Black Elk wasn't sure.
But he did the dance,
and then he had a vision.
He saw the spotted eagle,
the tree full of flowers,
and men in special shirts.

Later, he made the shirts
for some of his people.
On his own shirt
he painted a spotted eagle.
The people went on dancing
and hoping for the new world.

Above: Indian warriors in costume. Below: Most of
these Indians were killed at Wounded Knee Creek.

Instead, soldiers came.
On December 29, 1890,
they attacked the Indians
near Wounded Knee Creek.

Most of the Indians
were women and children.
They were trying to hide
in a deep gulch
when the soldiers shot them.

Two famous Sioux chiefs: American Horse (left) and Red Cloud

After the battle of
Wounded Knee Creek (above),
the dead Indians were buried
in a mass grave (right).

Black Elk and others
fought the soldiers.
But it was no use.
There were too many.

Later that day, snow fell
and a white blanket covered
the women and children.
Black Elk never forgot them.
He said his people's dream
died there at Wounded Knee.

Black Elk (left) with John Neihardt

Chapter 5

An Old Man's Story

Many years later,
Black Elk met a writer,
John Neihardt.

He liked Neihardt.
He said he would tell
him about his life
and his great vision.
Later, Neihardt would put
it all into a book.

BLACK ELK SPEAKS

Being the Life Story of a Holy Man of the Oglala Sioux

as told through
JOHN G. NEIHARDT
(Flaming Rainbow)

Introduction by
VINE DELORIA, JR.

University of Nebraska Press
Lincoln and London

Black Elk (center)
with John Neihardt (left)
and Standing Bear (right),
who made the drawings
for Neihardt's book
Black Elk Speaks.
The first page
of the book is
shown at left.

Black Elk talked
for a long time.
Then he said he wanted
to go to the mountain
he had seen in his vision.

They went on a sunny day.
No rain had fallen
for many weeks.
Black Elk stood
on the mountain and prayed
to the Great Spirit.

"All things belong to you,"
he said, ". . . the two-leggeds,
the four-leggeds,
the wings of the air,
and all green things that live.
O make my people live!"

Clouds gathered
as the old man prayed.
Raindrops mixed with
the tears on his face.
Then Black Elk was silent
and the sun shone again.

Important Dates

1863	December—Born on the Little Powder River to Black Elk and White Cow Sees
1873	Had a great vision
1876	Battle at the Little Bighorn River
1882	Became a medicine man
1886-89	Traveled in Europe
1890	Massacre at Wounded Knee
1931	Told life story to John Neihardt
1950	Died on Pine Ridge Reservation, South Dakota

INDEX

Page numbers in boldface type indicate illustrations.

PHOTO CREDITS

ABOUT THE AUTHOR

Carol Greene has degrees in English Literature and Musicology. She has worked in international exchange programs, as an editor, and as a teacher. She now lives in St. Louis, Missouri, and writes full-time. She has published more than eighty books. Others in the Rookie Biographies series include *Benjamin Franklin, Pocahontas, Martin Luther King, Jr., Christopher Columbus, Abraham Lincoln, Robert E. Lee, Ludwig van Beethoven, Laura Ingalls Wilder, Jackie Robinson, Jacques Cousteau, Daniel Boone, Louis Pasteur*, and *Elizabeth the First*.